D0854361

A KINGFISHER TREASURY OF

Bible Stories
Poems *and*
Prayers
for Bedtime

That in his light
We may see light

A KINGFISHER TREASURY OF

Bible Stories
Poems *and*
Prayers
for Bedtime

Selected and retold by Ann Pilling

Illustrated by Kady MacDonald Denton

KING*f*ISHER

For David and Lorna,
Lydia and Naomi,
with much love (A.P.)

For Gina Pollinger (K.M.D.)

KINGFISHER
An imprint of Kingfisher Publications Plc
New Penderel House, 283-288 High Holborn, London WC1V 7HZ
www.kingfisherpub.com

First published by Kingfisher 1990
as *Before I Go To Sleep: Bible Stories, Poems and Prayers for Children*
This edition first published in hardback by Kingfisher 2000
This edition first published in paperback by Kingfisher 2001

2 4 6 8 10 9 7 5 3 1
1TR/0901/TIMS/FR(FR)/140MA

A CIP catalogue record for this book is available from the British Library.

ISBN 0 7534 0649 7

Printed in China

ACKNOWLEDGEMENTS

The publisher would like to thank the copyright holders for permission to reproduce the following copyright material:

The Bodley Head, on behalf of the Estate of Ruth Sawyer for *Christmas Morn* from THE LONG CHRISTMAS
by Ruth Sawyer; Jonathan Cape Ltd., on behalf of the Estate of Laurence Housman for *Light looked down* from
THE LITTLE PLAYS OF ST. FRANCIS by Laurence Housman; The Church Missionary Society for *Lord of the Loving
Heart*; Grafton Books, a division of the Collins Publishing Group, for *O God, who made the small nest of the wren* and
Once upon a time there was a man who was a miracle from THE GOLDEN COCKEREL BOOK OF MORNING
READNGS by M.E.Rose; Methuen and Co. for *An Old Woman of the Roads* by Padraic Colum from an ANTHOLOGY OF
MODERN VERSE; The Reverend Peter Midwood for *A Swaledale Parish Prayer*; Peterloo Poets for *What the Donkey Saw* by
U.A. Fanthorpe from POEMS FOR CHRISTMAS; Ann Pilling for *Dear God, we thank you* and *Dear Lord*,
copyright © ANN PILLING 1990, SCM Press for *A Prayer from Prison* by Dietrich Bonhoeffer from LETTERS AND
PAPERS FROM PRISON, THE ENLARGED EDITION, 1971; Unwin Hyman Ltd. for *Bread* by Freda Elton Young, from
THE BOOK OF A THOUSAND POEMS by H.E. WILKINSON.
Extracts and psalms are taken from the King James Version of the Holy Bible and the Book of Common Prayer,
except Psalm 107 from THE NEW ENGLISH BIBLE 2nd Edition © 1970, reprinted by permission of
Oxford & Cambridge University Presses; and Psalm 40 adapted from various sources by Ann Pilling.

*Every effort has been made to trace and contact copyright holders. Should any omission have occurred, the publisher
will be happy to make the necessary correction in future reprintings.*

God be in my head,
And in my understanding;
God be in mine eyes,
And in my looking;
God be in my mouth,
And in my speaking;
God be in my heart,
And in my thinking;
God be at mine end,
And at my departing.

The Sarum Primer

Contents

THE OLD TESTAMENT

THE NEW TESTAMENT

THE OLD TESTAMENT

Now thank we all our God
With heart and hands and voices,
Who wondrous things hath done,
In whom his world rejoices;
Who from our mother's arms
Hath blessed us on our way
With countless gifts of love,
And still is ours today.

M. Rinkart

God Makes the World

IN the beginning, God made the heaven and the earth. But at first the earth was shapeless and empty, and everything was covered with thick darkness.

So God said, "Let there be light!" And there was light. God saw that it was good, so he separated it from the darkness. He called the light "Day" and the darkness "Night".

Then God made the sky over the great waters that covered the earth, gathering them together in one place so that dry land appeared. And on this land he set plants and trees growing, and it all seemed very good.

Then lights were put in the sky like great lamps, the sun, the moon and the stars, to give us the seasons and to make night and day. Into the sea God put all kinds of fish, and birds to fly above them in the air. "Have young," he said to them all, "and fill this earth of mine to overflowing."

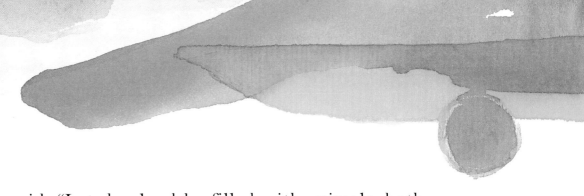

Then he said, "Let dry land be filled with animals, both large and small, those that walk and creep, and jump and run." And it all seemed very good indeed.

At last, God made Man himself, and Man was special, because he looked like God. He was so special he was put in charge of all the things that now filled the marvellous new world, the plants and the herbs, the trees and their fruits, the fish and the birds, and all the creeping, running, jumping things. And God blessed him.

"Rule the earth and its creatures which I have made," he said. "They are for you."

Then God looked all around and felt that Creation was very good indeed. It had taken six long days to make it, so on the seventh day he rested.

And that is why the seventh day of the week is a holy day, because it is when God rested from all his work.

Genesis 1–2

Glad that I live am I,
 That the sky is blue;
Glad for the country lanes
 And the fall of dew.
After the sun the rain,
 After the rain the sun;

This is the way of life
 Till the work be done.
All that we need to do,
 Be we low or high,
Is to see that we grow
 Nearer the sky.

Lizette Woodworth Reese

*O God, who made the small nest of the wren and
the great sky of the stars, we thank thee that
thou art in all things, great and small. Amen.*

M. E. Rose

The Snake in the Garden

THE very first man that God ever made was called Adam and for him, in a place called Eden, he planted a most beautiful garden. It had four great rivers flowing through it, and flowers and trees of every kind. Two trees were special, the Tree of Life and the Tree of the Knowledge of Good and Evil, which grew right in the middle. "You may eat fruit from any of the trees," God said, "except from the Tree of the Knowledge of Good and Evil. If you do that, then you will die."

So Adam lived in Eden, ruling over its animals and giving them all names. But he was lonely, so God made a woman to live with him and share the garden. Her name was Eve.

One day an evil creature came slinking by and said to her slyly, "Did God really tell you not to eat from this special tree?"

"Yes," said Eve, "and if we eat from the Tree of the Knowledge of Good and Evil, or even touch its fruit, we will die."

"That's not true," the creature told her. "You won't die. God only said that because if you do eat from it, you will become like him, knowing both good and evil, as he does."

Then Eve, seeing how lovely the fruit was, and wanting to be wise like God, stretched out her hand, took the fruit and ate. And when Adam came he ate too.

In the cool of the evening God walked in his garden and came looking for them, but in their shame they had hidden away. So he called out to them and said, "Adam, Eve, did you eat fruit from the forbidden tree?"

"Eve gave it to me," answered the man.

"But it was that evil creature's fault," the woman explained. "He tricked me."

Then God said to the creature, "You will be punished for this. From now on you will be a snake that cannot walk upright, but can only crawl along the ground, and you shall eat nothing but dust." And the wretched snake slithered away.

Then he said to Adam and Eve, "I will not let you die, but from now on you must work, tilling the stony soil until it produces food for you to eat. It will be hard for you, my children, because it is full of weeds and thorns. But now that you have tasted of the Tree of the Knowledge of Good and Evil, you must leave this garden and live in the world." And they went sadly away.

Then God thought, "What if they should reach out and taste from the Tree of Life too? They would live for ever, then."

So, when he had cast them out of Eden, he put an angel there, and a flaming sword that turned this way and that, to guard the Tree of Life.

Genesis 2–3

Dear Lord,
Thank you that I am sometimes strong,
  help me when I am still weak;
Thank you that I am sometimes wise,
  help me when I am still foolish;
Thank you that sometimes I have done well,
  forgive me the times I have failed you;
And teach me to serve you and your world
  with love and faith and truth,
  with hope, grace, and good humour. Amen.

A Swaledale Parish Prayer

God who made the earth,
  The air, the sky, the sea,
Who gave the light its birth,
  Careth for me.

God who made the grass,
  The flower, the fruit, the tree,
The day and night to pass,
  Careth for me.

God who made the sun,
  The moon, the stars, is he
Who, when life's clouds come on,
  Careth for me.

Sarah Betts Rhodes

The Enormous Boat

NOAH was a good man, and walked with God, but the rest of the people had become very wicked. God was sad, but he was angry too, so he decided to bring a great flood upon the earth. But he wanted to save Noah and his family.

"You must build a huge wooden boat," God told him. "You must make it long and wide and tall, and paint it with tar so that the water can't get in. When it is finished you must shut yourself inside with your family, and into it you must take a pair of all the animals in my Creation, so that when the flood has gone down they can have young, to fill the earth again."

So Noah and his wife and their three sons set to work and built an enormous boat, exactly as God had said,

and when it was finished the animals came in, two by two: great lumbering elephants and long-necked giraffes, prickly old hedgehogs and nervous little mice, even a couple of tumbling furry kittens. And in through the windows flew birds of every kind: sparrows and thrushes, the raven and the turtle dove. When everyone was safe inside, God shut up all the doors and windows very tight. Then the rain came.

It rained for forty days without stopping once, and the whole earth turned into one enormous sea, filling the valleys and covering the mountain tops. Everything on earth was swept away and drowned, all except Noah and his family and his animals, snug and warm inside the enormous boat.

The flood waters boiled and bubbled and raged, but God did not forget Noah and at last he made a huge wind that blew across the earth, quelling the floods so that they began to go down. Little by little it stopped raining altogether, mountain tops broke the surface of the water and Noah's huge boat came to rest on top of Mount Ararat.

When all was calm, Noah opened a window and sent a raven out to see what was happening. When, after a week, it had not returned, he sent out a dove. But it came back very disappointed because no trees had appeared yet, so there was nothing to sit on. A few days later he sent it off a second time and this time it came back with a fresh green olive leaf in its beak. Then Noah knew that the flood really was over. Through his windows he could actually see dry land.

When he came out of the boat he built an altar to God, burning incense upon it to say thank you to him for sparing their lives. And when God smelled the sweet perfume, he was sorry he had brought the flood.

"I promise," he told Noah, "never to destroy my Creation again. While the earth remains, seedtime and harvest, cold and heat, summer and winter, day and night, shall not cease."

As a special sign of this promise he put a rainbow in the sky.

"Whenever I see it," he said, "I will remember what I have said, never to bring a terrible flood ever again."

So Noah and his family and all the animals went back safely into the world, and had children, so that the earth was full of living creatures, just as it had been before.

Genesis 6–9

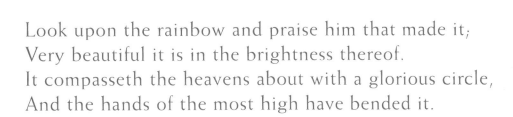

Look upon the rainbow and praise him that made it;
Very beautiful it is in the brightness thereof.
It compasseth the heavens about with a glorious circle,
And the hands of the most high have bended it.

Ecclesiasticus 43, v.11—12

The animals went in two by two,
  Hurrah! Hurrah!
The animals went in two by two,
The elephant and the kangaroo,
  And they all went into the ark
  For to get out of the rain.

The animals went in three by three,
  Hurrah! Hurrah!
The animals went in three by three,
The wasp, the ant and the bumble bee,
  And they all went into the ark
  For to get out of the rain.

The animals went in four by four,
  Hurrah! Hurrah!
The animals went in four by four,
The great hippopotamus stuck in the door,
  And they all went into the ark
  For to get out of the rain.

The animals went in five by five,
   Hurrah! Hurrah!
The animals went in five by five,
They warmed each other to keep alive,
   And they all went into the ark
   For to get out of the rain.

The animals went in six by six,
   Hurrah! Hurrah!
The animals went in six by six,
They turned out the monkey because of his tricks,
   And they all went into the ark
   For to get out of the rain.

The animals went in seven by seven,
   Hurrah! Hurrah!
The animals went in seven by seven,
The little pig thought he was going to heaven,
   And they all went into the ark
   For to get out of the rain.

Traditional

The Baby in the Basket

PHARAOH, the King of Egypt, was very worried. The Israelites, who lived as slaves in his kingdom, seemed to be growing stronger and cleverer with every day that passed. "What if they rise up against me?" he said to himself. "What if they make war on my people and drive them all away?" So he worked out a cruel plan to get rid of them all.

The plan was this: every baby boy born to an Israelite woman was to be thrown into the River Nile. Nothing could live very long in there, because it was full of crocodiles.

But one woman, who came from the family of Levi, was determined to save her little son from Pharaoh. The baby was strong and healthy and for three whole months she managed to keep him hidden.

The time came, however, when she could not hide her precious secret any longer. Someone was bound to find out about the baby sooner or later, and when they did he would be killed. So she wove a little basket out of rushes, made a lid for it and daubed it all over with clay and tar, to stop the water coming in. She put the baby inside and hid the basket in the tall reeds at the edge of the river. Then she crept away. But her daughter Miriam hid in the shadows, just to see what would happen.

Quite soon Pharaoh's daughter came along for her morning bathe, while her maids walked up and down the bank. As she knelt down she saw the funny little rush basket hidden in the reeds, and she sent one of her servant girls to bring it out.

When they opened it up they found a baby lying there. He started to cry when he saw all the strange faces.

"Why, this is a Hebrew child," the princess said, "poor little soul." She felt very sorry for him.

Just then, Miriam stepped out of her hiding place. "Shall I find someone to look after the baby?" she said cleverly, "One of the Hebrew women, perhaps?"

"Yes," said Pharaoh's daughter. "Go and fetch someone, quickly." So Miriam ran home and brought her mother back to her own little son, snug in his basket of rushes.

"If you will look after this child for me," the princess told her, "I will pay you good wages." So his mother took her little son into her arms again, and carried him safely home.

When he was old enough, however, Pharaoh's daughter took him to live with her in the royal palace, and he became her adopted son. She called him Moses because the name means "pulled out of the water".

Moses grew up to be one of the greatest of all the Israelites and it was he who led his people out of Egypt, where they had been slaves, back to the good land that God had always promised them, the land that overflowed with milk and honey.

Exodus 1–2

Hush, little baby, don't say a word,
Papa's gonna buy you a mocking bird.
If that mocking bird don't sing,
Papa's gonna buy you a diamond ring.
If that diamond ring turns to brass,
Papa's gonna buy you a looking glass.
If that looking glass gets broke,
Papa's gonna buy you a billy goat.
If that billy goat don't pull,
Papa's gonna buy you a cart and bull.
If that cart and bull turn over,
Papa's gonna buy you a dog named Rover.
If that dog named Rover don't bark,
Papa's gonna buy you a horse and cart.
If that horse and cart fall down,
You'll still be the sweetest little baby in town.

Traditional

Cradle Song

Sweet dreams, form a shade
O'er my lovely infant's head;
Sweet dreams of pleasant streams
By happy, silent, moony beams.

William Blake

Faithful Ruth

LONG ago there was a great famine in the land of Judah. A man called Elimelech, with his wife, Naomi, and their two sons, went to find food in a foreign country called Moab. While they were living there Elimelech died. Both the sons found wives for themselves. One was called Orpah and the other Ruth.

They lived in Moab for ten years, but then both the sons died too and old Naomi, left all alone, decided to go back to her own country of Judah. She had heard that God had blessed it with food again.

But she told Ruth and Orpah to go back to their own families. "You have been good to me," she said. "Now may God be good to you. May he bring you new husbands, and new homes." And she kissed them.

Then Ruth and Orpah wept bitterly. "Do not send us away," they pleaded.

But Naomi was firm. "Go back to your own people," she said, "for I am an old woman now. I have no sons left to be your husbands."

So, very sadly, Orpah said goodbye, but Ruth clung to Naomi. "Do not ask me to leave you," she said, "for where you go I will go too, and where you stay I will stay. Your people shall be my people, and your God my God.

Nothing but death will part us now."

So Ruth and Naomi travelled on together until they reached Bethlehem, just as the barley harvest was beginning. Ruth went into the fields to follow the reapers, hoping to pick up a few ears of corn that had been left behind.

Now all the land round about belonged to a very rich man called Boaz. He noticed the foreign girl gathering corn in his field and he asked his reapers who she was. "She came from Moab," they told him, "with old Naomi. She's been here since day-break, following us round and picking up the stray ears of corn."

Then Boaz called Ruth over to him and told her to stay close to his servants. "If you're thirsty," he said, "drink some of the water they have brought."

"But why are you so kind to me?" she said in amazement. "I'm just a foreigner."

"I have heard how good you have been to Naomi," he told her, "how you left your own home to be with her, and came instead to a strange land. May the Lord reward you, Ruth, for what you have done, the Lord God of Israel under whose wings you have taken refuge."

When the reapers stopped to eat, he made sure she had food too. "Don't scold her," he whispered to them, "but let her go among the barley sheaves and gather grain. In fact, drop some in her path deliberately, so that she has plenty."

When she got home again, Ruth told Naomi all about Boaz's kindness. "Blessings on him," said the old woman thankfully. "This shows that God still remembers us and cares for us, even now, when all our loved ones are dead." Then she told Ruth to tell Boaz that he was a relation of Elimelech, her dead husband. "Perhaps he will give us more help," she said.

So Ruth went off to find him, and when he heard what Naomi had said he told her to hold her cloak out wide. Into it he poured a great measure of barley, and she put it on her back and went home to show Naomi. "I believe that Boaz will not rest until he has done even more for us," the old woman told her.

And she was right, because Boaz sent for Ruth, and asked her to be his wife. In time she bore him a son. "Blessed be the Lord today," she told Naomi joyfully, "he did not leave you alone. This grandson has come to give you new life, and comfort in your old age. And I, your daughter-in-law, who loved you so dearly, have done more for you in the end than all your sons!" Then Naomi took her little grandson, and held him very close.

The neighbouring women called the baby Obed, and he became the father of Jesse, who in turn became the father of King David. And it was from this great family that Jesus himself was born. That is why he was sometimes called "the Son of David".

Ruth 1—4

An Old Woman of the Roads

Oh, to have a little house!
    To own the hearth and stool and all!
The heaped-up sods upon the fire,
    The pile of turf against the wall.

To have a clock with weights and chains
    And pendulum swinging up and down,
A dresser filled with shining delph,*
    Speckled and white and blue and brown.

I could be busy all the day
    Clearing and sweeping hearth and floor,
And fixing on their shelf again
    My blue and white and speckled store.

I could be quiet there at night,
    Beside the fire and by myself,
Sure of a bed, and loth to leave
    The ticking clock and the shining delph.

Och! but I'm weary of mist and dark,
    And roads where there's never a house or bush,
And tired I am of bog and road,
    And the crying wind and the lonesome hush.

And I am praying to God on high,
    And I am praying him night and day,
For a little house, a house of my own –
    Out of the wind's and the rain's way.

Padraic Colum

*pottery

May the road rise to meet you,
May the wind be always at your back,
May the sun shine warm on your face,
The rain fall softly on your fields;
And until we meet again,
May God hold you in the palm of his hand.

A Gaelic Blessing from Ireland

The Boy Who Killed a Giant

DAVID was a shepherd boy, the youngest son of a man called Jesse. He was handsome and strong, and he was brave too, for wild animals had come prowling round his flocks at night and David had killed them with his bare hands. He could also play wonderful tunes on his harp, and when King Saul had wild and terrible dreams, he would send for David so that the boy might sing songs to him. The soft sweet music always sent the king to sleep. Saul loved David very much, and though he was just a shepherd, he became the king's special armour-bearer too.

Now King Saul and his Israelites had been fighting a long fierce war with the Philistines, and once more the two armies were facing each other, this time across a deep valley. From the Philistines' camp strode a huge man called Goliath. He wore a massive bronze helmet and a clanking coat of chain mail, and his spear was as thick as a great tree trunk.

"Send a man out to fight me!" he bellowed. "If I kill him,

you will all become our slaves!" At the sound of his voice the Israelites quaked in terror; no one dared move an inch.

Morning and evening, for forty days, Goliath came and jeered at the terrified soldiers. David, who was up in the mountains looking after his father's sheep, heard about it and secretly wondered what to do. Then his father Jesse gave him some food to take to his brothers, who were soldiers in King Saul's army. While he was talking to them, Goliath appeared yet again.

"Come and fight!" he yelled. But all the Israelites ran away.

David alone knew that God was on their side, and he told the king that he would fight the giant himself.

"Oh no," Saul said in dismay. "He is a great warrior and you are a mere boy."

But David answered, "The God who saved me from the lion and the bear will surely save me from Goliath." When he heard this the king said, "Go, and may the Lord be with you," and he gave David armour, a coat of mail, a helmet and a sword.

Everything was so heavy that the boy could hardly walk, so he took it all off, picked up his shepherd's crook instead, and chose five smooth pebbles from the bed of the stream. He tucked them into his knapsack with his little leather sling, then he set off to meet the giant.

Goliath sneered horribly when he saw a young boy approaching. "Am I a dog," he screamed, "that you bring nothing but sticks to beat me with? Come on then, I'll soon finish you off, and when you're dead I'll feed your body to the crows."

But David replied, "You may have a spear and a javelin but I have the power of Almighty God, the Lord, the one on whom you have turned your back. Goliath, it is you who will die today, that all the earth may know that there is a God in Israel."

As the giant rushed upon him, David took one of his little pebbles, fitted it into the sling and fired it straight at Goliath's forehead. It struck him so hard that it sank deep into the flesh and the huge man was soon rolling dead at David's feet.

And from that day on David lived in the royal palace and became the special friend of Jonathan, the king's son. And Jonathan loved him as he loved his own soul.

1 Samuel 16–17

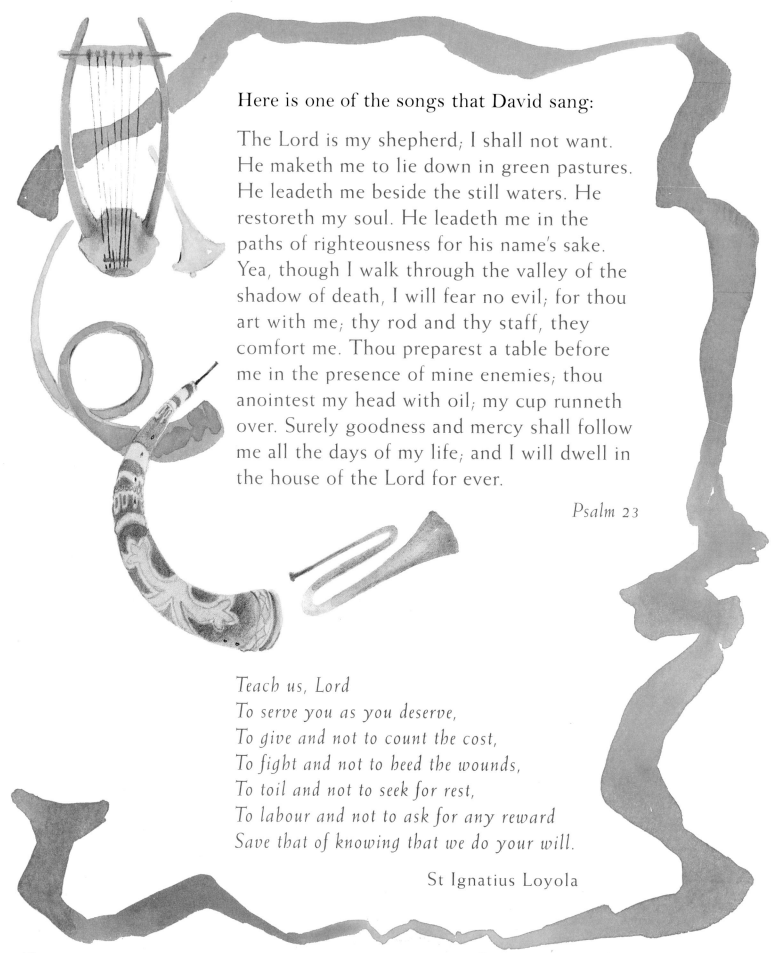

Here is one of the songs that David sang:

The Lord is my shepherd; I shall not want. He maketh me to lie down in green pastures. He leadeth me beside the still waters. He restoreth my soul. He leadeth me in the paths of righteousness for his name's sake. Yea, though I walk through the valley of the shadow of death, I will fear no evil; for thou art with me; thy rod and thy staff, they comfort me. Thou preparest a table before me in the presence of mine enemies; thou anointest my head with oil; my cup runneth over. Surely goodness and mercy shall follow me all the days of my life; and I will dwell in the house of the Lord for ever.

Psalm 23

Teach us, Lord
To serve you as you deserve,
To give and not to count the cost,
To fight and not to heed the wounds,
To toil and not to seek for rest,
To labour and not to ask for any reward
Save that of knowing that we do your will.

St Ignatius Loyola

The Amazing Flour Barrel

ELIJAH was a holy man from Gilead and God had given him a very special gift; he was able to look into the future and see what was going to happen.

One day, in a dream, he saw that the rain would stop falling for months on end, and that there would be a terrible famine. Then he heard the voice of God telling him to prepare for a very long journey. "Go east," said the voice, "until you find a little stream that flows near the River Jordan. It will provide water for you to drink, and I have commanded ravens to bring you food."

So Elijah did what God had said. He found the little stream and drank from it, and sure enough, each morning and evening the ravens carried food down to him in their beaks.

But in the end even the little stream dried up, and Elijah became very thirsty. "Now go to the city of Zarephath," God commanded. "There is a woman living there who will look after you." So Elijah set off again and came at last to the gate of the city, where he saw a poor woman gathering a few sticks to make a fire.

"Could you bring me some water?" he asked her. "And a little food? I have walked so many miles today." But the woman said bitterly, "I have hardly any food left, only a handful of flour in a barrel and a tiny drop of oil in a jar. These sticks are to make the fire for my very last meal. When that's gone I shall die, and so will my poor son."

"Don't be afraid," Elijah told her. "Go home and make your fire. But when the food is cooked bring me a little too. God has promised that your barrel of flour and your jar of oil will never be empty, not until it rains again."

So she went home and did exactly what he had told her. And it was true: there was always oil in the jar and flour in the barrel. God had kept his word.

But even though they now had enough to eat, her son fell ill, wasted away, and died. In her grief the poor woman turned on Elijah, the stranger. She blamed him. "Why did you bring this on me?" she wept. "Did you simply come here to remind me of the mistakes I've made in my life, and to punish me for them?"

Very patiently, Elijah gathered the boy in his arms, took him upstairs and laid him on his own bed. Then he prayed to God, long and hard. "Why has this awful thing happened," he said, "to a poor woman who took me in and looked after me? Dear Lord, bring her child to life again, I beg you."

And God heard his prayer. Very soon the boy started to breathe again, opened his eyes and sat up. Elijah took him down to his mother. "He is alive," he said.

Then the woman held her son very tight. "Now I know you are a true man of God," she said joyfully, "a special person through whom he shows his power and his love." Through Elijah, God had turned her darkness into light.

1 Kings 17

Lord, make me an instrument of your peace.
Where there is hatred, let me sow love,
Where there is injury, pardon,
Where there is despair, hope,
Where there is darkness, light,
Where there is sadness, joy.

St Francis of Assisi

The Friendly Lions

IN the days of King Darius there was a man in his court called Daniel. He was a fine man who walked with God, and the king liked and trusted him. He was planning to put him in charge of the whole kingdom. But the royal servants were deeply jealous and they were watching Daniel very carefully.

Their problem was that Daniel did nothing wrong at all, and they soon realized that the only way to get him into trouble was to make a new law to trap him. They knew he was a very holy man, and faithful to his God, so they wrote out a special decree which said that from now on people could only pray to the king. Anybody who disobeyed would be thrown into a pit full of lions.

Now Daniel heard about this new law, but he took no notice. Three times a day he went off to his house, opened the windows so that he could look towards Jerusalem, fell on

his knees and prayed. The jealous servants spied on him, then rushed off to tell the king what they had seen. "Doesn't the new law say that prayers may only be offered to you," they said slyly, "and that anyone who disobeys must be thrown to the lions?"

"It is true," admitted King Darius, though his heart was heavy. "It does say that, and a royal law cannot be changed."

"Well, Daniel is taking no notice," they informed him. "He prays to God three times a day. We've seen him."

When the king heard this he was very unhappy, because he loved and honoured Daniel, and all day he thought hard for some way to save him. But the jealous servants came back again and told him firmly that the new law could not be changed.

So Darius gave orders for Daniel to be thrown to the lions. "But may your God, whom you serve so faithfully, save you now," he said, as Daniel was dragged away from the palace to the deep pit where the savage creatures were waiting.

The servants rolled a huge stone over the entrance and the king came and marked it with his own special ring, to show that nobody must break in.

Then he went back to his palace. For the rest of the day he neither ate nor drank and he sent away his court musicians. All night he lay tossing and turning, and thinking about Daniel.

In the morning he woke very early, ran to the pit and called out in fear, "Daniel, servant of the living God, has the one whom you served so faithfully been able to save you from the jaws of the lions?"

And from deep in the pit a voice rang out. "O King," it said, "may you live for ever. In the night, God sent his angel to shut the lions' mouths. He knew I was innocent, and that I had done you no harm."

Darius was overjoyed to hear him and he ordered his men to bring Daniel up out of the pit. They could find no marks on his body at all. That was because he had trusted in God with his whole heart to save him.

As for the jealous servants who had tricked him and tried to have him killed, they were thrown into the pit themselves. Even before they had reached the bottom all the lions sprang up and devoured them whole.

And the king wrote a grand decree, for every nation upon earth, bidding all people to fear and honour Daniel's God. "For he is the living God," he said. "He delivered my dear servant Daniel from the lions' jaws, and his Kingdom shall last for ever and ever."

Daniel 6

Out of the Pit

I waited patiently for the Lord;
He bent down to me, and heard my cry.
He brought me up, out of the muddy pit,
Out of the clay and the quicksand,
And set my feet upon a rock.
He has put a new song in my mouth,
A song of praise to our God.

from Psalm 40

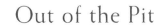

*Dear Lord, You have done such wonderful things.
You looked after Daniel, and I know you will
look after me. Amen.*

Ann Pilling

THE NEW TESTAMENT

Light looked down and beheld Darkness.
  "Thither will I go," said Light.
Peace looked down and beheld War.
  "Thither will I go," said Peace.
Love looked down and beheld Hatred.
  "Thither will I go," said Love.
So came Light and shone.
  So came Peace and gave rest.
So came Love and brought Life.
  And the Word was made flesh* and dwelt among us.

Laurence Housman

This is how St John describes the birth of Jesus.

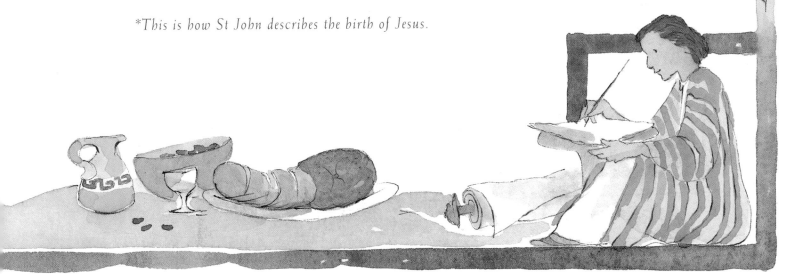

I Sing of a Maiden

I sing of a maiden
That is makeless;*
King of all kings
To her son she chose.

He came all so still
Where his mother was,
As dew in April
That falleth on the grass.

He came all so still
To his mother's bower,
As dew in April
That falleth on the flower.

He came all so still
Where his mother lay,
As dew in April
That falleth on the spray.

Mother and maiden
Was never none but she;
Well may such a lady
God's mother be.

Unknown

*matchless

Mary

THERE was once a young girl called Mary. She lived in Galilee in a town called Nazareth and she was soon to marry a carpenter called Joseph.

But one day God sent Gabriel, the greatest angel of all, to give her some very important news. She was troubled when she saw him, and wondered what on earth he could want with her.

"Greetings, most favoured one," he said, "and do not be afraid. You have found favour with God. Very soon you are going to have a baby. You must call him Jesus. He will be great, the Son of the Most High. God will give him the throne of David, his mighty ancestor, and he will reign for ever and ever."

But Mary was puzzled. "I am not even married," she told the angel.

"The Holy Spirit will come down to you," Gabriel said, "and God's own power will rest upon you; therefore, that holy thing which you shall bear will be called the Son of God. Nothing is impossible with him."

"I am his servant," Mary whispered. "May it happen just as you have said." And Gabriel went away.

But when she was alone she lifted up her voice and rejoiced.

"Tell out, my soul, the greatness of the Lord,
Rejoice, O my soul, in God my Saviour,
Who has looked so tenderly upon his humble servant.
For from this day all people shall call me 'blessed',
The Lord has dealt with me so wonderfully."

Luke 1

No Room

JUST a few days before her baby was born, Mary had to go on a long journey with the carpenter Joseph. Everyone had been ordered to pay a special tax in their home town, and his home was in Bethlehem.

Just as they arrived, Mary knew that her baby was going to be born; but there was no room for them in the inn. All they were offered was a stable, and that is where the Son of God was born. There was no lovely silk-lined cot for him, only a manger full of hay, with the animals standing around.

That night some shepherds who were out guarding their sheep on the hills near Bethlehem were startled by a great light in the sky. An angel came down and told them not to be afraid. "I bring you good news of great joy," he said, "news for everyone on earth. Christ the Lord has been born tonight.

If you go now, you will find him wrapped in swaddling clothes, lying in a manger."

And suddenly the whole sky was filled with angels, hundreds upon thousands of them, all praising God. "Glory to God in the highest," they sang, "and on earth peace, good will towards all people."

"Come on," the shepherds said to each other, when at last the angels had gone away. "Let's go to Bethlehem and see for ourselves." So they rushed off and found Mary and Joseph, and baby Jesus lying in a manger, exactly as the angel had said.

Luke 2

What the Donkey Saw

No room in the inn, of course,
And not that much in the stable,
What with the shepherds, Magi, Mary,
Joseph, the heavenly host –
Not to mention the baby
Using our manger as a cot.
You couldn't have squeezed another cherub in
For love or money.

Still, in spite of the overcrowding,
I did my best to make them feel wanted.
I could see that the baby and I
Would be going places together.

U. A. Fanthorpe

54

Dear God, We thank you that your tiny son,
born in a stable, had a heart big enough
to embrace the whole world. Amen.

Ann Pilling

The Three Kings

MEANWHILE, in his great palace in Jerusalem, jealous King Herod had been talking to some wise men. He was alarmed, and frightened, because he had heard about the baby that had been born in Bethlehem and he feared that the child would one day seize his throne. The prophets had said that a great king, the "Messiah", would be born in that little town.

"Where is this baby who is going to be King of the Jews?" the wise men asked Herod. "We have seen his special star in the east and we want to go and worship him."

"You'll find him in Bethlehem," Herod said. Then he added cunningly, "But be sure to let me know when you get there. I want to come and worship him too."

So off they went, following the star; and it led them all the way to Bethlehem, where it stopped, hovering over the place where Jesus lay. They were overjoyed to see the star there and they went straight in. Out of their great store of treasures they gave the baby gifts, gold and frankincense and myrrh. But they were not so foolish as to return to Herod. In a dream God had warned them to find a different way home.

In another dream, God gave a warning to Joseph. "Go to Egypt," his angel said, "and stay there till I tell you all is safe. King Herod is plotting to kill your baby son."

So Joseph got up immediately and stole away by night with Mary and their child, for the far-off land of Egypt.

Herod flew into a great rage when he realized that the wise men had tricked him. He gave a cruel command that all the young children in and around Bethlehem should be killed. That way he could be sure that Jesus would die too.

But Joseph and Mary were already safe in Egypt, and they did not go back again until Herod was dead and they knew it was safe. Then they settled in the town of Nazareth, with Jesus.

God was looking after his precious son most carefully; he was going to do such wonderful things when he grew up.

Matthew 2

Christmas Morn

Shall I tell you what will come
to Bethlehem on Christmas morn,
who will kneel them gently down
before the Lord new-born?

One small fish from the river,
with scales of red, red gold,
one wild bee from the heather,
one grey lamb from the fold,
one ox from the high pasture,
one black bull from the herd,

one goatling from the far hills,
one white, white bird.

And many children – God give them grace,
bringing tall candles to light Mary's face.

Ruth Sawyer

Jesus in Trouble

WHEN Jesus was twelve years old, Mary and Joseph went up to Jerusalem as usual, for the great feast of the Passover, and took their son with them. When it was all over, they set off for home again, travelling with a big group of friends; but Jesus stayed behind. They had gone a whole day's journey before they realized he was missing. Then they began to hunt anxiously amongst all their friends and relations. But Jesus was nowhere to be found.

Off they trudged, all the way back to Jerusalem. But it was a big, bustling city and they spent three days looking for him. Finally they spotted him in the Temple, sitting in the middle of all the Jewish teachers, asking all kinds of questions and listening carefully to their answers. Everyone who heard him was amazed at his deep understanding, and at how much such a young boy knew.

His parents were astonished to find him there, and Mary could not hide her distress. "My son," she said, "why have you treated us like this? Your father and I have been terribly worried; we've looked everywhere for you."

"But why did you look for me?" Jesus asked them calmly. "Didn't you know that I had to be in my Father's house, doing my Father's work?" But neither of his parents understood what he was saying.

Together, they all returned home to Nazareth, and after this their young son was much more obedient. But Mary never forgot what had happened in the Temple, treasuring the memory in her heart.

As for Jesus, he grew taller and stronger, and he grew in wisdom too. People loved him, but nobody loved him as much as his Father in heaven, in whose house he had lingered when he was just twelve years old.

Luke 2

My Best Friend

Jesus, friend of little children,
    Be a friend to me
Take my hand and ever keep me
    Close to thee.

Teach me how to grow in goodness,
    Daily as I grow:
Thou hast been a child, and surely
    Thou dost know.

Never leave me, nor forsake me;
    Ever be my friend;
For I need thee, from life's dawning
    To its end.

Walter J. Mathams

A Marvellous Picnic

EVERYBODY wanted to meet Jesus, and to hear his wonderful stories, and wherever he went huge crowds followed him. Once, when he had been preaching all day, he said to his special friends, the disciples, "Let us go away by ourselves now, to some lonely place, so that you can all get some rest." So they set off in a boat to find somewhere really quiet and peaceful.

But the people had all rushed ahead of them and the minute Jesus stepped on shore everybody crowded round eagerly. His heart filled with love for them then; they were like sheep who had lost their shepherd, and although he was very tired he started preaching again.

The day wore on and on and his friends began to worry. "It's getting late," they said, "and this is such a lonely place. Send the people away now to the villages round about to buy themselves something to eat."

"You feed them," Jesus replied.

"How on earth can we buy food for so many?" one of them wanted to know. "There must be about five thousand people here." Then another came up and said, "There's a lad here, Master, with five barley loaves and two fish. But that won't go very far."

"Make everybody sit down," Jesus commanded, so they all settled themselves on the grassy slopes in little groups.

Then he took the loaves and the fish, looked up to heaven and gave thanks, then passed the food to his disciples to give to the hungry people. Everyone ate till they were quite satisfied and at the end of the meal there were enough crumbs and bits of fish left over to fill twelve baskets. It was the most marvellous picnic ever.

I think that boy with the loaves and the fish must have remembered it all his life, don't you?

Matthew 14; Mark 6; Luke 9; John 6

Bread

Be gentle when you touch Bread.
Let it not lie
Uncared for,
Unwanted.
So often Bread
Is taken for granted.

Beauty of patient toil,
Wind and rain
Have caressed it.
Christ often blessed it.
Be gentle when you touch Bread.

Freda Elton Young

The Big Storm

On the day of the marvellous picnic it was late in the afternoon when Jesus finally sent the people away. He told the disciples to get into their boat and sail home ahead of him, while he went into the hills to pray.

When evening came he was still alone. The boat was a long way from land by this time, and a really bad storm had blown up. The waves were crashing against the side of the boat, and the wind was howling. All night, the disciples had to struggle to hold their course.

Very early next morning, long before sunrise, Jesus came to find them, walking across the water. When they saw what he was doing they cried out in terror, "It's a ghost." But he calmed them at once, saying, "Take heart, it is I. Do not be afraid."

Peter, his chief disciple, said, "Lord, if it really *is* you, command me to walk on the sea as well."

"All right," Jesus replied. "Come," and he held out his hand.

So Peter climbed out of the boat and tried to copy Jesus. But when the wind began to buffet him this way and that, and the great waves hurled themselves at him, his courage failed and he began to sink. "Lord, save me!" he shouted. And Jesus immediately caught him by the hand, saying, "Peter, how little your faith is. Why did you have any doubts?"

Together they got back into the boat, and the great storm died away completely. The disciples knelt down and worshipped Jesus. "You really are the Son of God," they said.

Later that day they landed at a place called Gennesaret. As soon as people knew who had arrived, they came flocking to him, bringing all their sick friends and relations. They believed they needed only to touch the hem of Jesus' robe to be made well again. And that is exactly what happened.

Matthew 14; Mark 6; John 6

Dear God, Be good to me.
The sea is so wide,
and my boat is so small.

The Breton Fisherman's Prayer

Others there are who go to sea in ships
    and make their living on the wide waters.
These men have seen the acts of the Lord
    and his marvellous doings in the deep.
At his command the storm wind rose
    and lifted the waves high.
So they cried to the Lord in their trouble,
    and he brought them out of their distress.
The storm sank to a murmur
    and the waves of the sea were stilled.
Let them thank the Lord for his enduring love
    and for the marvellous things he has done for men.

from Psalm 107

They Wanted to See Jesus

ONCE, when Jesus was on his way to Jerusalem, he heard a loud voice crying his name. It was a blind beggar called Bartimaeus who'd asked people in the crowd what all the fuss was about. "Why, Jesus of Nazareth is passing by," they had told him, and the minute he heard that he yelled at the top of his voice, "Jesus, Son of David, have mercy on me!"

Those at the front of the crowd ordered him to be quiet but he only shouted more loudly, "Son of David, have mercy on me!"

Jesus stopped and commanded those nearby to bring Bartimaeus to him. "What do you want me to do for you?" he asked.

"Lord, let me see," the poor man pleaded.

"Receive your sight," Jesus told him. "Your faith has healed you." At once the man could see and he followed the Master, glorifying God for the great miracle.

Soon afterwards Jesus was passing through Jericho. There was a very rich man in that city called Zacchaeus, a tax collector. He wanted to see Jesus too, but he was very short

and the heads of the crowd were in the way. Nobody let him through; they didn't like tax collectors very much.

So he ran on ahead and climbed up into a sycamore tree, knowing that Jesus would pass right underneath. When Jesus reached the tree he looked up into the branches and saw the little man hanging there, looking eagerly down.

"Hurry up and climb out of there, Zacchaeus," he said. "I'm coming to stay at your house today."

Zacchaeus scrambled down, overjoyed, but the crowd muttered, "Huh, Jesus has gone to stay at the house of a wicked, greedy man."

But the tax collector knew he had done bad things. "Lord," he told Jesus, "I'm going to give half my goods to the poor, and if I've cheated anyone, I'll give them four times what I owe."

Jesus said, "Today salvation has come to this house. I, the Son of Man, have come to find what is lost, and to save it."

That day, Zacchaeus was truly saved.

Mark 10; Luke 18–19

I never saw the moor,
I never saw the sea;
Yet know I how the heather looks,
And what a wave must be.

I never spoke with God,
Nor visited in heaven;
Yet certain am I of the spot
As if a chart were given.

Emily Dickinson

Zacchaeus was a very little man,
And a very little man was he.
He climbed up into a sycamore tree
For the Saviour he wanted to see.
And when the Saviour passed that way,
He looked into the tree and said:
"Now, Zacchaeus, you come down,
For I'm coming to your house for tea."

from Junior Praise

Lost and Found

THE ordinary folk loved Jesus dearly but the rich and powerful ones were jealous. "He spends too much time with bad people," they muttered. "He sits and eats with liars and cheats. We don't understand it at all."

"Let me explain," Jesus said. "If you had a hundred sheep and one of them wandered away, wouldn't you leave the ninety-nine safe in their pasture and go hunting for the lost one until you found it? When you had, you would lift it up on to your shoulders and carry it home in triumph; then you would call all your friends and neighbours together and say, 'Look at this, I've found my lost sheep. Let's have a party.' What I'm saying is that there will be more joy in heaven over a sinner who says he's sorry than over the good people who don't need to." And to show them exactly what he meant he told them a story about a man and his two sons.

The younger son liked having a good time, and one day he said to his father, "I want my share of your property now." The father agreed and divided what he had between his two sons. A few days later the younger son left home and settled in a land far away, where he spent the money on drinking and gambling. In no time at all he had used up every penny.

When his pockets were empty a dreadful famine spread over the countryside and very soon he began to need food. So he went to work for one of the local landowners, who packed him off into one of his fields to feed the pigs. He was now so hungry that he would have been quite glad to eat some of the pig swill. But nobody gave him a thing.

In the end he came to his senses. "My father's servants back home have more food than they can eat," he told himself, "and here I sit, about to collapse with hunger. I will get up this minute and go to my father and I'll say to him, 'Father, I've sinned against God and against you too. I'm not fit to be called your son any more. Treat me as one of your hired servants.'" And he got up and started for home.

But his father saw him while he was still a long way from the house and his heart went out to him. He ran towards him with arms outstretched, flung them round the boy's neck and kissed him. "Father," the son said, thoroughly bewildered, "I've sinned against God and I've sinned against you as well. I'm not fit to be called 'son' any more. Treat me as one of your hired servants."

But his father seemed not to be listening; he was too busy giving orders. "Bring the best robe," he commanded, "and put it on my son. Put a ring on his finger and shoes on his feet, then go and kill my prize calf. We're going to have a feast. My 'dead' son is alive again, my 'lost' son has been found." And everyone began to celebrate.

Now the older son had been out working in the fields and as he walked back he heard music and dancing. When the servants explained what was going on, he was so angry he refused to go in.

Out came the father and begged his son to join them, but he was still in a rage. "Look," he pointed out, "I've slaved for you all these years and I've never once disobeyed you. But you never killed a prize beast for me, no, not so much as a goat kid, so I could feast with my friends. But the minute *he* turns up, having squandered all the money you gave him, you go and kill the prize calf. It's not fair."

"My son," said his father, "you are always with me, and whatever I have is yours. But how could we not rejoice on such a happy day? Your brother, whom I'd given up for dead, is alive and well. I thought he was lost, but he's been found."

And in the same way, Jesus told the people round him, the angels of God sing aloud for joy when one sinner comes home, saying he is sorry.

Luke 15

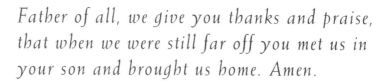

Father of all, we give you thanks and praise,
that when we were still far off you met us in
your son and brought us home. Amen.

The Alternative Service Book

Love

Love bade me welcome; yet my soul drew back,
   Guilty of dust and sin.
But quick-eyed Love, observing me grow slack
   From my first entrance in,
Drew nearer to me, sweetly questioning
   If I lacked anything.
"A guest," I answered, "worthy to be here."
   Love said, "You shall be he."
"I, the unkind, ungrateful? Ah, my dear,
   I cannot look on Thee."
Love took my hand, and smiling did reply,
   "Who made the eyes but I?"
"Truth, Lord, but I have marred them: let my shame
   Go where it doth deserve."
"And know you not," says Love, "who bore the blame?"
   "My dear, then I will serve."
"You must sit down," says Love, "and taste my meat."
   So I did sit and eat.

George Herbert

The Man on a Donkey

ONCE, a clever lawyer who had been listening to Jesus' stories decided to try and trick him. "Teacher," he asked, "what must I do if I want to live for ever in God's Kingdom?"

"What does it say in the Scriptures?" Jesus answered. "It says that you must love God with all your heart, with all your soul, with all your mind and with all your strength. After that you must love your neighbour as much as you love yourself."

"You're right," Jesus told him. "Do this and you will have everlasting life."

But the lawyer wasn't satisfied. "Who is my neighbour?" was his next question.

"There was once a man travelling from Jerusalem to Jericho," Jesus said, "and on a lonely stretch of road some robbers attacked him. They stripped him, beat him up and went off, leaving him half dead.

"Now as it happened a priest soon came along the same bit of road. But when he saw the poor man lying there,

he simply crossed over to the other side. Some time later another priest, a Levite this time, also came walking along. He did exactly the same thing, just crossed the road and hurried on his way.

"Eventually a Samaritan rode up, someone you wouldn't expect to be any help at all. But when he saw the man, pity filled his heart. He went straight over to him, poured oil and wine on to his wounds and bandaged them up; then he lifted the poor man on to his own donkey and took him to the nearest inn, where he looked after him all night.

"In the morning the Samaritan took out his purse and gave the innkeeper some money. 'Take care of him,' he said, 'and if you spend any more than this, I'll pay you when I come back.'

"Now which of these three people was 'neighbour' to the man who had been attacked by robbers?" Jesus asked.

"The one who was kind to him," the clever lawyer replied.

"Go and do as he did, then," said Jesus.

Luke 10

Lord of the loving heart,
May mine be loving too.
Lord of the gentle hands,
May mine be gentle too.
Lord of the willing feet,
May mine be willing too.
So may I grow more like thee
In all I say and do.

Unknown

Two Precious Gifts

ONE day Jesus was preaching in the Temple. Looking up, he caught sight of all the rich people dropping their offerings into the charity chest. Then he saw a poor widow come along, slip in two small copper coins and creep away.

At once, he called his disciples to him and told them what he had seen. "That poor woman gave more than anyone else," he said. "Though the others were rich, they simply gave money that they would not miss. In her poverty she gave everything she had in the world."

Soon after this someone else came along with a special gift; this time it was for Jesus. He was eating a meal with a friend called Simon and a woman suddenly entered the house carrying an alabaster jar of very expensive ointment. Everyone in the town had heard about this woman and all the bad things she'd done. But she loved Jesus very much.

Opening the jar, she poured all the ointment over Jesus' head, and the house was filled with its sweet smell. Then, kneeling down before him, she began to weep bitterly because of all the wrong she had done. As her tears fell on to his feet, she wiped them away with her hair.

The people standing round were indignant to see the wasted ointment, and Judas, the disciple in charge of the money, stepped forward. "That could have been sold for a great deal," he pointed out, "and the money could have been given to the poor."

"Don't be angry with her," Jesus said. "She has done a beautiful thing to me. You will always have the poor with you, but you will not always have me. Besides, in pouring this ointment over me she has prepared my body for burial." Jesus knew already that very soon he would be put to death.

Then he turned to the master of the house. "Simon," he said, "when I came in from the dusty street you offered me no water for my feet, but this woman has bathed them with her own tears, and wiped them with her hair. You gave me no kiss, but she has been kissing my feet since the minute I entered. You did not anoint my head with oil; she did. Her many sins have been forgiven, because of her great love.

"Woman," he said, reaching down to her, "your faith has saved you. Go in peace."

Matthew 26; Mark 14; Luke 7; John 12

What can I give him,
    Poor as I am?
If I were a shepherd
    I would bring a lamb;
I were a wise man
    If I would do my part;
Yet what I can I give him –
    Give my heart.

Christina Rossetti

Lord
isn't your creation wasteful?
Fruits never equal
the seedlings' abundance.
Springs scatter water.
The sun gives out
enormous light.
May your bounty teach me
greatness of heart.
May your magnificence
stop me being mean.
Seeing you a prodigal
and open-handed giver
let me give unstintingly
like a king's son
like God's own.

Archbishop Helder Camara

They All Ran Away

WHEN Jesus rode into Jerusalem, on a little donkey, crowds lined the streets, with everybody cheering and waving palm branches. But this made the important men of the city, the chief priests and the scribes and the rulers of the Temple, very frightened. The people were flocking to Jesus in such large numbers that they feared he would become the ruler instead of them, perhaps even a king. These jealous men did not understand that when Jesus spoke of his "kingdom", he meant the Kingdom of God. They decided that they must get rid of him, once and for all.

Jesus already knew that they were planning to put him to death. It said so in the ancient Scriptures which he had read and studied since he was a child.

On the night before the chief priests came to arrest him, he went with his disciples to the Mount of Olives. "Before very long, Peter," he said to his oldest friend, "you will deny that you ever knew me."

"Never!" Peter reassured him, and so did all the others.

"Yes," Jesus repeated, "before the cock crows you will

deny me three times." He knew that they would all be very frightened when the men came to take him away.

Then he told his friends to keep watch, while he went away by himself, to pray. But it was very late and, one by one, they all fell asleep. "Couldn't you stay awake for a single hour?" he said to them, when he found them all lying on the ground; then he returned to his prayers. But the second time he came back, and the third, he found them fast asleep again. "Still sleeping?" he said to them as they all got up, heavy-eyed, not knowing what to say. "Come, make yourselves ready. The traitor is here." People were making their way through the darkness with lanterns, looking for him.

It was Judas, one of his own disciples, who had brought these people to Jesus. They had paid him thirty pieces of silver for doing so. Up they came, armed with swords and clubs, as if Jesus were some kind of robber. Judas had arranged a secret sign, to show them whom to arrest. "I will kiss him," he had told them.

"Hail, Master," he said, putting his arms round Jesus, and they immediately closed in and grabbed him.

"Do you betray the Son of Man with a kiss?" Jesus asked his disciple. Then the rest of his disciples ran off in terror, and Jesus was taken away to Caiaphas, the High Priest. But Peter stayed, following at a distance, to see what was going to happen.

He sat in the courtyard, warming himself by the fire there, while they asked Jesus all kinds of questions, in an attempt to trick him, but Peter noticed that his Master hardly answered a word. While they were questioning him they spat at him, and struck him across the face.

A maid came up to Peter and said, "You were one of Jesus' friends, weren't you?" But Peter shook his head. "I'm sure this man was with Jesus of Nazareth," she told the people standing by. But Peter swore that he was not. "But you were," they all said, "we can tell from the way you speak."

"I do not know the man," Peter said savagely. And immediately the cock crowed.

Then the Lord turned round and looked at Peter, and he remembered what had been said on the Mount of Olives, that before the cock crowed he would deny Jesus three times. And he went out, and wept bitterly.

Matthew 21–26; Mark 11–14; Luke 19–22; John 12–18

A Prayer from Prison

Lord Jesus Christ
You were poor and in distress,
a captive and forsaken as I am.
You know all man's troubles;
You abide with me
when all men fail me;
You remember and seek me;
It is your will that I should know you
and turn to you.
Lord, I hear your call and follow;
Help me. Amen.

Dietrich Bonhoeffer

The Great Darkness

In the morning the rulers of the Temple decided that Jesus must die. So they dragged him in front of Pontius Pilate, a Roman governor, who was in charge of Jerusalem and of the lands round about. "Are you the King of the Jews?" he said.

"You say I am," Jesus replied. But apart from that he said nothing at all.

Now at that time it was the great feast of the Passover, when it was the custom for the governor to set a prisoner free. The people were allowed to choose who it should be. In the jail there was a wicked man called Barabbas. Pilate asked them if they wanted him to go free. Or would they prefer Jesus?

While he was discussing it with them, his wife sent him a message. "Have nothing to do with that innocent man Jesus," it said. "In my dreams last night I was deeply troubled because of him." But the people who had brought Jesus to the governor were quite determined to have him killed. "Let him be crucified!" they all shouted.

"Why? What has he done wrong?" Pontius Pilate asked them. But they just shouted, "Crucify him!" louder and louder. In the end he had to let Barabbas go free, and Jesus was taken away.

Then it was the turn of the Roman soldiers. They made Jesus wear a kingly robe, to mock him, and they pushed a crown of thorns down on to his head. They put a cane in his hand, pretending it was a royal sceptre, then they hit him and jeered at him, until the time had come for him to be taken out to be crucified.

The custom was that each man carried his own cross up to the hill of Golgotha (which means "place of a skull").

But Jesus stumbled and fell, so they got a man called Simon of Cyrene to carry it for him. When they had nailed Jesus to his cross they sat round arguing about who should get his clothes. They couldn't agree, so in the end they threw dice to decide.

Two robbers were crucified with Jesus, one on each side of him. One hurled insults at him. "If you really are the Christ," he said, "then save yourself, and save us too." But the other rebuked him "Don't you fear God?" he said. "You got the same sentence as he did. So did I and we both deserved it. But this man has done nothing wrong at all." Then he said, "Lord Jesus, remember me when you come into your Kingdom."

"Today, you will be with me in paradise," said the Lord.

At about twelve o'clock, as the three of them hung dying, there was a sudden darkness over the whole earth. It lasted for three long hours, and in the Temple the holy curtain was split in two, from the top to the bottom. Then Jesus cried out, "Father, into your hands I give my spirit." And he died.

When the Roman officer who was on watch saw what had happened, he was filled with wonder. "Truly," he said to himself, "this man was the Son of God."

Matthew 27; Mark 15; Luke 23; John 18–19

Were you there when they crucified my Lord?
Were you there when they crucified my Lord?
Oh, sometimes it causes me to tremble, tremble, tremble;
Were you there when they crucified my Lord?

Were you there when they nailed him to the tree?
Were you there when they nailed him to the tree?
Oh, sometimes it causes me to tremble, tremble, tremble;
Were you there when they nailed him to the tree?

Were you there when they laid him in the tomb?
Were you there when they laid him in the tomb?
Oh, sometimes it causes me to tremble, tremble, tremble;
Were you there when they laid him in the tomb?

Traditional

When I survey the wondrous Cross
On which the Prince of Glory died,
My richest gain I count but loss,
And pour contempt on all my pride.

Isaac Watts

The Great Sun

WHEN evening came a rich man called Joseph, from Arimathaea, who had also been a follower of Jesus, went to Pontius Pilate and asked if he could have the Lord's body. It was given to him and he took it away, wrapped it in clean fresh linen, then laid it in a tomb cut out of the rock. Then he rolled a huge stone across the entrance, and went away. Mary Magdalene, who had once anointed Jesus with oil, and Mary, the sister of his friend Lazarus, sat watching.

Meanwhile, the men who had Jesus put to death went to Pontius Pilate themselves. "Sir," they said, "when he was alive that liar Jesus of Nazareth claimed that three days after his execution he would rise from the dead. You ought to make sure the tomb is properly guarded, just in case his disciples steal the body, then tell the people he has risen."

"You may have some soldiers," Pontius Pilate told them. "Go and make it as secure as you can." So they went off to the tomb, sealed the stone all round and set a guard to keep watch.

Early in the morning of the third day the two Marys went back to see Jesus' grave. Suddenly there was a tremendous earthquake and an angel came down from heaven. He rolled back the enormous stone and sat on it. His face was like lightning and his robes were as white as snow. When they saw him, the guards shook in terror and fell down, fainting.

Then the angel said to the two women, "Do not be afraid. I know you are looking for Jesus, who was crucified. He is not here, he has risen, just as he promised. Look, this is where his body lay.

"Now go quickly and tell his disciples that he has indeed risen from the dead and gone on ahead into Galilee. You will see him there. This is the message I was sent to give you."

Still nervous, but with great joy in their hearts, the women hurried away from the tomb and ran to find the disciples. Suddenly Jesus met them on the path. He greeted them, and they fell down on their faces before him and clasped his feet.

"Do not be afraid," he said, "but tell my friends that they must go to Galilee. They will see me there, up on the mountainside."

So the disciples made their way to Galilee, to the place where Jesus had said he would meet them. There he was, just as he had promised, and when they were all gathered together he gave them a special command.

"God my Father has given me full power," he told them, "in heaven and on earth. Your task is to go out and find disciples among every nation, baptizing them in the name of the Father and the Son and the Holy Spirit, teaching them to obey all the things I have commanded you.

"And remember, I am with you always, even unto the end of the world."

Matthew 27–28

There are also many other things which Jesus did. If they were all to be put down, I suppose the earth itself could not contain all the books that would be written.

John 21

Once Upon a Time

Once upon a time there lived a man who was a miracle,
Once upon a time there grew a man like God;
All the people came to him to listen to his teaching,
Children gladdened at his touch, and men grew good.

Blind girls blinked their eyes awake and saw the world all
    coloured;
Crooked men stood straight as trees, alive and strong;
Lonely people lifted up their hearts like flowers to sunshine,
Crippled children danced for joy, and dumb boys sang.

Always I am with you, said this man who was a miracle,
I will never leave you till the seas run dry;
Listen for me, look for me, and you will surely find me;
And the wonder of my touch will bring you joy.

M. E. Rose

INDEX OF POEMS AND PRAYERS